CONTENTS

Introduction   **5**

Physically   **6**

Mentally   **9**

Spriritually   **14**

Conclusion   **17**

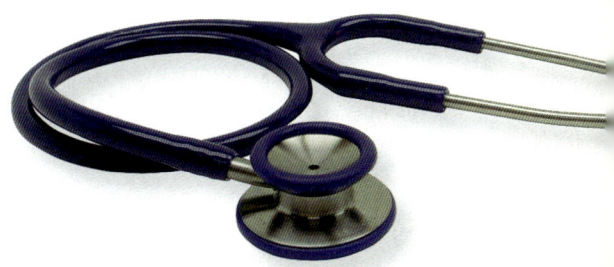

'Hurry, Worry, Bury' is the epitaph for many people in this century.'

The increasing number of patients taking tranquillizers; the rising incidents of stress diseases; the frequency of attempted suicide, which has reached epidemic proportions; all these reflect sadly on our modern society and demand an answer. I have no doubt that a proper regard for the LORD's Day would help to ameliorate these problems. Speaking as a physician, there are good reasons physically, mentally and spiritually why we should set aside the first day of the week as a special day unto the LORD. The ancient promise still holds true:

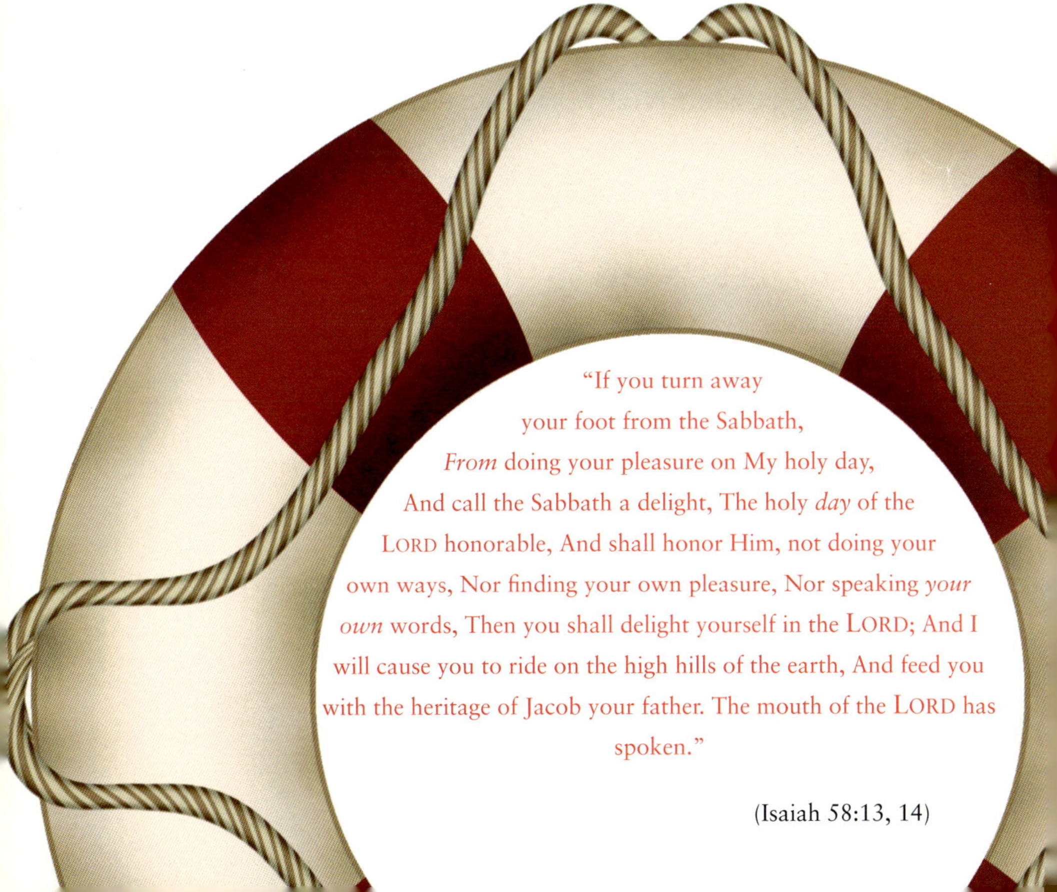

"If you turn away your foot from the Sabbath, *From* doing your pleasure on My holy day, And call the Sabbath a delight, The holy *day* of the LORD honorable, And shall honor Him, not doing your own ways, Nor finding your own pleasure, Nor speaking *your own* words, Then you shall delight yourself in the LORD; And I will cause you to ride on the high hills of the earth, And feed you with the heritage of Jacob your father. The mouth of the LORD has spoken."

(Isaiah 58:13, 14)

Physically

'There are natural, in-built laws which govern human behaviour'.

An obvious example is that you cannot continue to work without sleep indefinitely. After a certain number of hours, you fall asleep, whatever you are doing. In a torture situation where people are forcibly kept awake, there comes a break point when they crack up catastrophically. There are many examples of 24-hour cycles in the body (called circadian rhythms), showing the natural functioning of the body on a daily basis. Your temperature varies by two degrees; many chemicals in the blood stream alter in their concentration; and your ability to concentrate fluctuates in a cyclical manner. You can test the last by keeping awake all night—at around 6 a.m. you begin to 'wake up', even though you have not been asleep! Similarly, there are weekly cycles. It is significant that the natural split of the year is in lunar months (4 x 7 days) rather than calendar months. From time to time, societies have tried to extend the working week to eight days or ten days. Each attempt has failed. The natural variation is six days' work, one day rest. The body cries out physically one day in seven for rest and change. At the University of Leeds, we have measured for several months in a working man the 17-oxogenic steroids in his urine. These chemicals are breakdown products of the hormones from the adrenal gland. High volumes occur with stress and activity. There was a weekly rhythm of these chemicals in the urine. The lowest levels were on a Sunday. It is not clear whether this was an inherent rhythm, or whether it was a reflection

'The body cries out physically one day in seven for rest and change.'

100%

of decreased stress and activity. Whichever it was, it demonstrates the beneficial effect of a weekly day of rest. This is one reason why responsible union leaders are opposed to Sunday trading. They recognise that their members need a day of rest. Once legislation permits the opening of shops on a Sunday as a general principle, storekeepers who do not wish to open seven days a week will be forced to do so if they wish to remain competitive. The burden of extra work will fall on the employees—and not only must this mean higher prices, but shop workers will be subjected to even more unsocial hours and physical pressure.

'... shop workers will be subjected to even more unsocial hours and physical pressure.'

Mentally

The poet once wrote:
**What is this life if full of care
We have no time to stand and stare?**

He appreciated that to get the best out of life, we needed time to relax mentally. We need time to unwind from the tensions of the week, whether these are produced by the frustrations of a repetitious job, or by the demands of an administrative position. Doctors have to treat many illnesses which are categorised as 'stress diseases'. These include peptic ulcer, muscular rheumatism, migraine, hypertension (raised blood pressure), and coronary heart disease. Stress is not the only factor. Very often there is a constitutional predisposition, shown by a family history of the

Doctors have to treat many illnesses which are categorised as 'stress diseases'.

same condition. Nevertheless, as the sufferers are only too well aware, stress plays an important part in precipitating attacks.

Animal experiments by Professor Hans Selye, a pathologist of Montreal, have provided confirmatory evidence, suggesting that these stresses affecting the mind produce many hormones from the adrenal glands, and these, in turn, harm the body.
God's provision of a day of rest helps

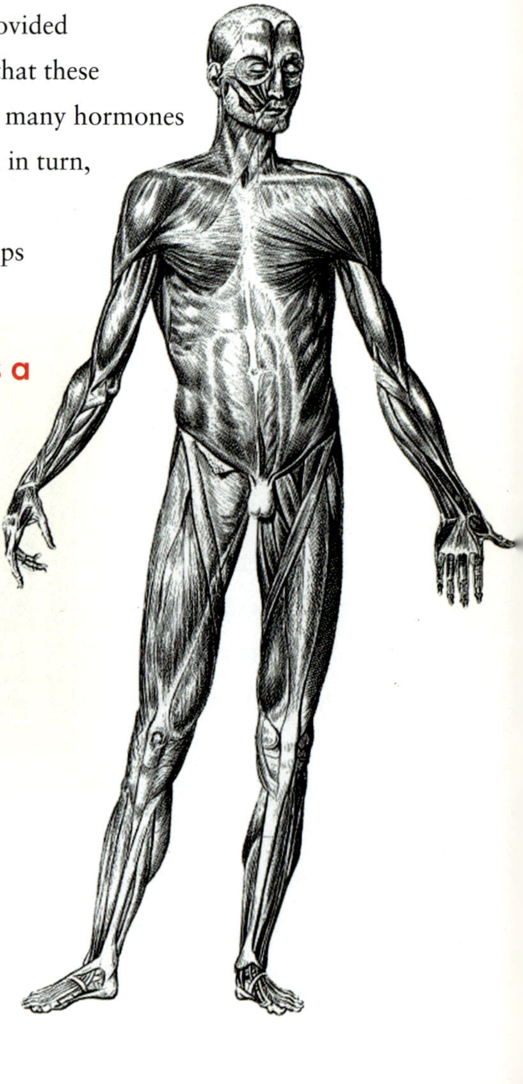

**A Sabbath well spent brings a week of content
And health for the toils of tomorrow;
But a Sabbath profaned, whate'er may be gained,
Is a certain forerunner of sorrow.**

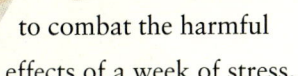

to combat the harmful effects of a week of stress. The verse of Sir Matthew Hale, a former Lord Chief Justice, remains even more true today than when first written—see poem on left-hand page:

As a university teacher, I warn my students against over-studying before exams and in particular advise them not to revise on Sundays. The most striking and sad case we had was a student who worked throughout Sunday, and took amphetamines to keep himself awake as he remorselessly revised through the night. He sat down to the exam on Monday and spent three hours covering sheet after sheet of paper with nothing but his name. The brain is an amazing computer which God has programmed to need one day's rest in seven. That is not a rash analogy. There is suggestive evidence that most dreams are the computer ditching rubbish. Your own experience will tell you that

'often the solution to a problem comes when you have laid it to one side and you are relaxing ...'

then out of the blue the answer comes to your consciousness. The computer has been working, uncluttered by the additional data and signals you are trying to feed it. That is why Archimedes leapt out of his bath shouting 'Eureka!' It was while he was relaxing in the warmth of the water that his great principle came. Intense, single-minded concentration is not the best stimulus for creative thinking. We need that one-in-seven time to set our mind on other things.

George Nachman painted a delightful piece in the Chicago Tribune. He wrote, not as a Christian, but as a shrewd observer.

One weekend, recently, I looked out the window and discovered that Sunday had disappeared. Nobody had swiped it exactly, but something had gone out of the noble day. Suddenly, I realised what it was: Sunday had turned into Tuesday. Out on the street, people no longer were strolling about. They had direction, a midweek glint in their eyes that meant business. They were walking briskly in and out of stores instead of browsing quietly past the windows. The scene was as busy as your average workaday Tuesday, throwing the whole week out of whack.

'Sunday was the only day you could be legitimately lazy, since nobody else was getting a whole lot accomplished either.'

Now Sunday is just another day, and it appears to have lost its real purpose. Back in the old days, Sunday had character. It was prim, but underneath it had a certain toughness, some confidence and a sense of security. It was the most sturdy and unflappable of days, one people could count on. You did not market; you did not go to the office for a few hours; you didn't even hunt for antiques. One of the things you definitely did not do was go downtown and buy sheets in a sale.

But just try lying around the house on Sunday now—knowing that half the world is out there doing things. Even people who claim to be relaxing are jogging and exercising like mad. So you see, we truly do need Sunday back the way it was, as a weekend cushion—unless Sunday has simply outlived its usefulness and people just plan to proceed from Saturday into Monday without that placid old day-long hammock in between.

Spiritually

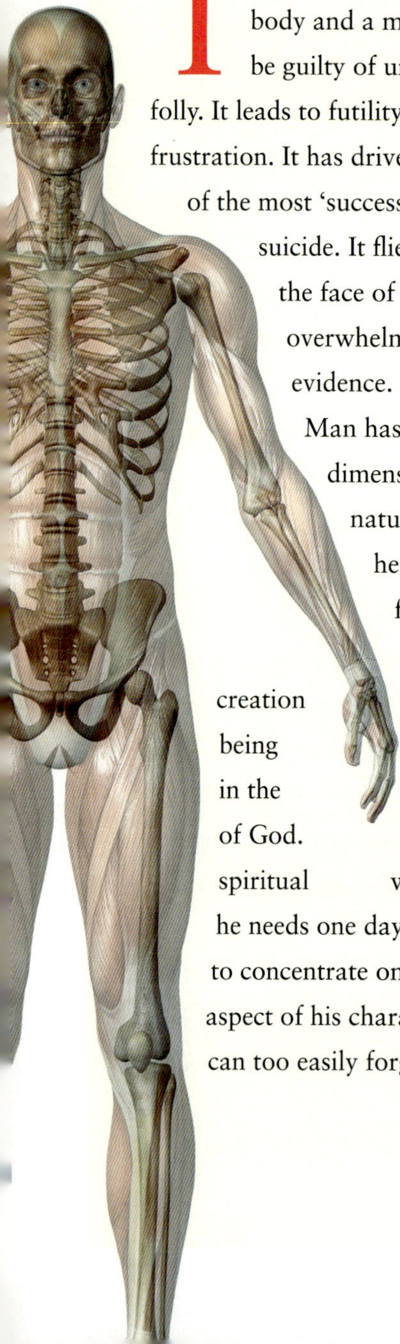

To live as if man is just a body and a mind is to be guilty of unutterable folly. It leads to futility and frustration. It has driven many of the most 'successful' to suicide. It flies in the face of overwhelming evidence.

Man has a spiritual dimension to his nature. Indeed he is distinct from the animal creation in being made in the image of God. For his spiritual wellbeing, he needs one day in seven to concentrate on this vital aspect of his character. We can too easily forget that 'healing' and 'holy' come from the same root. Since God made us in toto, he certainly knows what is best for us as individuals and as a society. No one quibbles with the prohibition on stealing, lying, coveting, murder—nor even in

'Man has a spiritual dimension to his nature'.

their honest moments with the command 'You are not to commit adultery', despite our permissive age with its epidemic of veneral disease and broken homes. Why should we argue with the command that we are to keep holy the Sabbath day?

A man told me it was needlessly

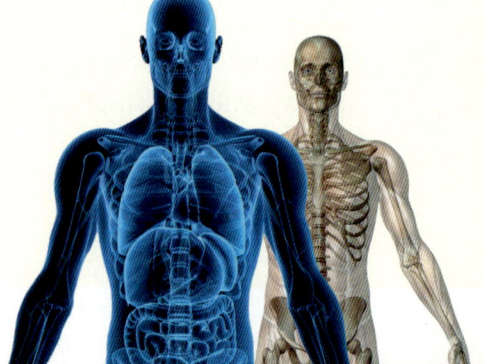

> 'True freedom is not the liberty to do what you like, but the ability to be what you were meant to be and the power to do what you ought'.

restrictive. Yet it is no more needless than the law which forbids you to drive up the right hand side of the M1, or to mainline with heroin for pleasurable purposes. Restrictions are necessary for our welfare and the benefit of others. True freedom is not the liberty to do what you like, but the ability to be what you were meant to be and the power to do what you ought. Physically, mentally and spiritually there are bounds within which we must live if we are to fulfil our destiny. Within that fence, we have an almost endless variety of possibilities for freedom. That is why it says of the Lord Jesus Christ, 'His service is perfect freedom.'

A man said to me recently, '"The Sabbath was made for man, not man for the Sabbath." Surely that means man can do what he likes on a Sunday.'

Perhaps I may illustrate the problem and solution in this way. I am driving along a clear road early one morning. As I approach a set of 'Keep Left' bollards, a child darts

out from the pavement. The only way I can avoid the child is to drive to the right of the bollards. I do so unhesitatingly because the bollards were made for man, not man for the bollards. Yet as a general rule I still keep to the left of the bollards. Jesus himself delineated the two clear areas of exception, works of necessity and works of mercy. I will go into hospital to see a patient of mine who has developed a medical problem on Sunday, but I will not accept invitations to teach general practitioners taking postgraduate courses on the LORD's Day.

'But I thought we lived under grace, not under law,' another man said to me.

It is true that our salvation is entirely of grace. I may keep the Sabbath meticulously, but it will not save me. I trust entirely in the redeeming work of Christ upon the cross for my salvation, not pleading a single good deed to

'That is why it says of the LORD Jesus Christ, 'His service is perfect freedom'.

merit favour with God. Justification is by faith alone. But that does not mean I ignore the law. Apart from being my schoolmaster to lead me to Christ, it provides the guiderails for my Christian living. Indeed the teaching of Jesus sharpens the law; it doesn't dispense with it. Adultery is now in a look, not just an act. Murder comes down to the harbouring of hatred in the heart. Nevertheless, the motive for keeping the law is different. Let me illustrate the point again: I drove to a friend in Norfolk who lived in a stately home. In the built-up areas, I restricted my speed to 30 miles per hour (especially when I saw a police car in my rear view mirror!). As I turned into the drive leading up to the hall, no speed limit applied, since I was off the main road. Nevertheless I kept well below 30 miles per hour, because I knew my friend appreciated those who drove slowly through the grounds. Love was an even more powerful influence in keeping me below the limit than the law. In other words, love fills the loopholes of the law as Romans 13:10 advocates. God has made it perfectly clear what he desires as far as the Sabbath day is concerned. Out of love for him I wish to obey. I find, as it happens, that this is to my best advantage also. God is no man's debtor.

God has made it perfectly clear what he desires as far as the Sabbath day is concerned.

Conclusion

From a medical point of view, one day set apart for rest and worship is best for man physically, mentally and spiritually. The Creator God who made man in his own image certainly had man's welfare at heart when, from the beginning of creation, he instituted the weekly Sabbath. The fourth commandment underlined its importance.

We ignore the Sabbath at our peril. We keep it to our inestimable benefit.

Sport and Sundays
Dan Walker

ISBN 978-1-84625-172-6
Large-format booklet, colour throughout, 32pp

Dan Walker is a successful sports journalist who currently works for a major UK broadcaster. He is also a Christian who firmly believes that Sunday is the Lord's Day, a day for rest from work and for worship of God. Why does he believe this? Did he have to compromise his beliefs in order to be successful in his career? Here he tells his story, from his childhood right up to the present day. It is a testimony to the truth of God's promise in 1 Samuel 2:30: 'those who honour Me I will honour'.

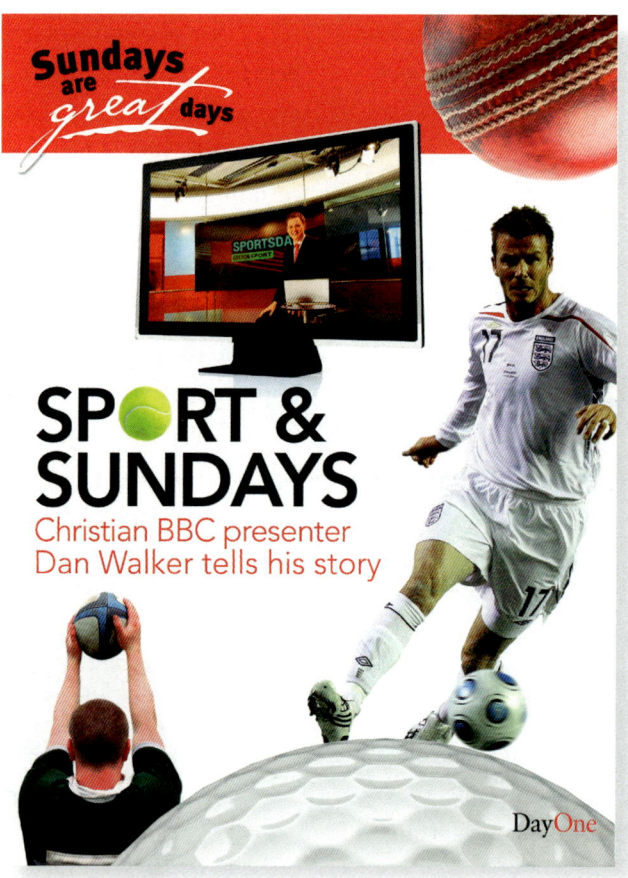